W9-AJQ-670

Colin Powell

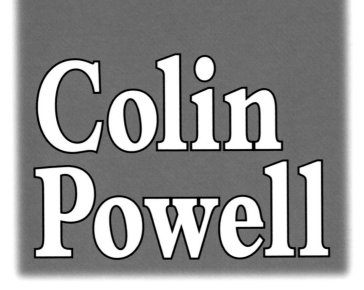

Colin Powell

Reggie Finlayson

3 1489 00372 1956

Bナ #19.95

Lerner Publications Company • Minneapolis

To my parents, William and Edith Finlayson,
who have always seemed heroic to me

Front cover: Powell speaks to families of soldiers killed in the Persian Gulf War.

Back cover: Powell addresses the crew of the USS *Wisconsin.*

Copyright © 1997 by Reggie Finlayson

All rights reserved. International copyright secured. No part of this book may be reproduced or transmitted in any form or by any means, electronic or mechanical, including photocopying and recording, or by any information storage or retrieval system, without permission in writing from Lerner Publications Company, except for the inclusion of brief quotations in an acknowledged review.

LIBRARY OF CONGRESS CATALOGING-IN-PUBLICATION DATA

Finlayson, Reggie.
    Colin Powell : people's hero / Reggie Finlayson.
        p.   cm.
    Summary: Traces the life and career of the Army general who became the country's first black chairman of the Joint Chiefs of Staff in 1989.
        ISBN 0-8225-2891-6 (alk. paper)
        1. Powell, Colin L.—Juvenile literature.   2. Generals—United States—Biography—Juvenile literature.   3. Afro-American generals—Biography—Juvenile literature.   4. United States. Army—Biography—Juvenile literature.   [1. Powell, Colin L.   2. Generals.   3. Afro-Americans—Biography.]   I. Title.
    E840.5.P68F56   1997
    355'.0092—dc20
        [B]   96–16740

Manufactured in the United States of America
1 2 3 4 5 6 – JR – 02 01 00 99 98 97

Contents

★ ★ ★ ★ 1

Will He or Won't He?

"A leader is someone you want to follow, if just out of curiosity."
—Colin Powell

A chill hung over much of the nation on November 8, 1995. It was the start of what would become one of the coldest, snowiest winters in American history. But most people weren't thinking about the weather. Instead, they were huddled around their televisions and radios waiting for the answer to a question.

"Will he or won't he?"

The question had stood unanswered for months. Now, America held its breath to hear the answer. Only one man could satisfy the curiosity of millions.

Retired General Colin Luther Powell, hero of Desert Storm—the Persian Gulf War, stepped to a cluster of microphones and stared into the bright lights and probing cameras of the American media. As he studied the crowd of reporters, he knew that the eyes of the entire nation were upon him. He was excited but not nervous. After a 35-year military career, the 58-year-old Powell was used to the pressures that accompanied power.

With his wife, Alma, beside him, Colin Powell announces his decision about the 1996 presidential race.

The crowd quieted and turned its attention to the speaker. Cameras flashed and pens were at the ready to record Powell's announcement about whether or not he would run for president of the United States. His family was with him. His wife, Alma, stood at his side, as she had for nearly every major decision of his adult life.

This decision had not come easily. It represented countless hours of consultation, heated discussions, and soul-searching. He considered his wife's misgivings and the passionate opinions of his adult children—two daughters and one son. He thought about the advice he'd gotten from former President George Bush. He thought about the many twists and turns his life had taken to bring him to this point. He thought, looked out, and spoke in measured tones:

> To offer myself as a candidate for president requires a commitment and a passion to run the race and to succeed in the quest—the kind of passion and the kind of commitment that I felt every day of my 35 years as a soldier, a passion and commitment that despite my every effort I do not have for political life, because such a life requires a calling that I do not yet hear.
>
> And for me to pretend otherwise would not be honest to myself, it would not be honest to the American people, and I would break that bond of trust. And therefore I cannot go forward. I will not be a candidate for president or for any other elective office in 1996.

The announcement shocked some people and saddened others. Potential rivals sighed with relief. Every poll showed that people would have voted for Powell. Republicans, Democrats, and independents all saw something in him they liked. Like a golden grizzly bear among the scrub pine, Powell towered above the other candidates. He had captured the hearts of the American people and excited their imaginations. Surprisingly, he had done so without ever declaring himself a candidate. People knew him by his actions, not by campaign promises.

During the 1991 war in the Persian Gulf, Americans often saw Powell on the nightly news. They admired the thoughtful way he sent young men and women into battle. He came to be known as a soldier who cared.

Colin Powell, an African American, never backed away from his ethnicity. He supported affirmative action, a system of recruiting minorities to schools and workplaces. He promoted the cause of blacks in the military. For these things he was beloved in minority communities. But he also attracted the support of southern whites and northern business leaders.

He had proven himself to be straightforward, honest, and well-spoken. Former President Gerald Ford called the retired, four-star army general one of the most eloquent speakers in the United States.

Powell greets American aviators at a base in Saudi Arabia during Operation Desert Storm.

Powell was the first African American in military history to serve as chairman of the Joint Chiefs of Staff—the highest ranking military post in the United States. He was also the first African American to serve as national security adviser, a staff member who reports directly to the president of the United States.

He's been decorated for outstanding military service in hot spots around the world, including Vietnam, where he was wounded in action. By all measures, General Powell is a hero of the people. This is his story.

11

Colin, about age five, on a visit to his aunt and uncle's house in Queens, New York

★ ★ ★ ★ 2

Kelly Street Hero

Colin Luther Powell was born in Harlem, New York, on April 5, 1937. His life began at the tail end of the Great Depression. Hard times hit everywhere in those days, and New York was no exception, especially in the African American community.

Jobs were scarce. Racial prejudice was strong. When there were jobs, African Americans were the last to be hired and the first to be fired. People pinched and saved the best way they knew how. But, too often, hard work just wasn't enough. Evictions were common. Soup lines got longer and longer.

The Powells were not a wealthy family, but they were luckier than most. At least they had a place to stay, food on the table, steady work, and a binding love. It was that love, generously shared, that impressed Colin from the beginning.

One day, when Colin was a small child in the care of his grandmother, he played a dangerous game. He plugged a hairpin into an electrical outlet. He saw a blinding light and felt a jolt that seemed to lift him off the floor. The sight scared his grandmother. She was frantic until she realized he was okay. Then she hugged and scolded him at the same time.

When his mother and father returned home that evening and learned what had happened, they reacted in much the same way. They fussed, scolded, and hugged all at once.

"My keenest memory of that day is not of the shock and pain," Powell often recalls, ". . . but of feeling important, being the center of attention, seeing how much they loved and cared about me."

His parents were Jamaican immigrants—Luther Theophilus Powell and Maud Ariel McKoy. They grew up near one another on the island nation but did not meet until moving to New York City in the early 1920s. They arrived separately but chased the same dream—the dream of a better life, shared by millions of other immigrants who came from Europe, Africa, and Asia. New York was a magnet.

Maud, who was known by family and friends as Arie, arrived in New York to join her mother, Alice McKoy, and a large clan of McKoys who had already settled in the United States. Arie came armed with a high school diploma.

Luther Powell had also attended high school in Jamaica. He was forced to find a job before he could graduate, however. He was the second of nine children born to a poor family. He took a job in a store, but it didn't offer many opportunities or rewards. So he packed up and moved. He worked his way to the United States on a United Fruit Company steamer.

When he stepped off the boat, he had little more than the clothes he wore. He had little money, but you couldn't really call him poor. He came to American shores with hopes, dreams, and ambitions. He was confident that with a fair chance, he could stand toe-to-toe with anybody in America.

Luther first worked as a gardener on estates in Connecticut and then as a building manager in Manhattan. Finally, he went to work in Manhattan's garment district, beginning in the stockroom of Ginsburg's, a clothing manufacturer. He was promoted to shipping clerk and eventually to foreman of the shipping department.

He was a small man who spoke with a West Indian accent. Though he was short, with each promotion he seemed to gain stature. When there was a dispute, relatives sought Luther's counsel. When there was trouble, they asked for his advice or financial support. Luther became the leader of his growing clan.

"His take-charge manner was reassuring," Colin wrote in his autobiography, *My American Journey.*

"Luther Powell became the Godfather, the one people came to for advice . . . for help in getting a job."

The family was the center of Colin's world. It was a happy world of warmth and security. It was a world in which "family members looked out for, prodded, and propped up each other." At the center of that world stood his parents.

Luther and Arie wanted the best for their two children, Colin and his older sister, Marilyn. Both parents worked hard and set money aside. Arie worked in the garment district as a seamstress.

Luther and Colin Powell, early 1940s

When Colin was four years old, the family left Harlem for Kelly Street in the South Bronx. The move marked a step up for the family. The South Bronx was a good place to live in the early 1940s. It was a clean, safe neighborhood. It had residents from almost every ethnic group in America. There were Italians, Jews, Hungarians, and blacks—just to name a few.

In the summer of 1950, Father Weeden, the priest at St. Margaret's Episcopal Church, chose 13-year-old Colin Powell to attend a church camp near Peekskill, New York. There were just a few openings, so the selection was an honor and a source of pride for the young man's family. Besides that, it offered an exciting change of pace from the hot summer streets of the South Bronx.

Colin was happy to go to camp. But shortly after arriving, he fell in with a bad group of boys. One night, under cover of darkness, the boys smuggled beer into the camp. They didn't think anyone had seen them as they returned with all the stealth of army rangers. They confidently hid the cans in a toilet tank to cool and returned to the other campers.

The boys were home free and felt triumphant as they mingled with the other campers. Each wore a smile of satisfaction, thinking they had a winning plan. But they weren't as smart as they thought.

It wasn't long before the priest in charge found the

beer and summoned all the campers to the meeting hall. He surveyed the young audience coolly before announcing his discovery. Backs stiffened throughout the hall as the boys considered the harsh discipline likely to flow from this incident. They silently braced themselves for the expected storm of words.

But the priest didn't threaten. He didn't even preach. He spoke in a quiet, firm voice. "Who will own up like a man?" he asked. The words hung there in the air like the breath on a cold day.

"Was that it?" Colin wondered. The possibilities flashed in his mind. He was sure no one had seen them. No one else knew who was guilty. All the boys had to do was keep quiet. Colin certainly didn't want to suffer the shame of getting caught. More than that, he had no wish to suffer his father's disapproval.

"Just keep quiet," he thought to himself.

But even as he thought it, the priest's words echoed in his mind with increasing volume. "Who will own up like a man? Who will own up like a man?"

Suddenly, things were very clear for Colin. Without further hesitation, he rose and said: "Father, I did it."

Two other boys surprised him by refusing to let him take the blame alone. Perhaps, inspired by his courage or some sense of loyalty, they stood to admit their part in the deed.

Justice was swift and merciless. The priest put the humiliated boys on the next train back to New York

City. It was a long and sad journey. But the worst part for Colin was the walk up Kelly Street to his house at 952. The buildings that usually made him feel secure seemed to press in on him. His shoulders ached. But that was just the beginning.

Bad news travels fast, and Colin's disgrace was on everyone's lips when he entered the family home. His mother attacked first. Her sharp questions cut deeper with each pass. Then his father joined in with his own angry words.

Colin could not help feeling ashamed. It seemed like he would carry the mark of a hoodlum or thug from that time forward. Never in his life had he felt as sad.

Just then, the telephone rang. It was Father Weeden calling for Luther. Colin watched as his father's grim face softened and even became friendly. He saw a reaction that gave him hope. Later, his father repeated what the priest had said, and his voice was full of joy:

"Yes, the boys had behaved badly," Father Weeden said. "But your Colin stood up and took responsibility. And his example spurred the other boys to admit their guilt."

His parents beamed. They were again proud of their son. Colin had not only shown good character but he also seemed to bring it out in others. He was, according to his father and mother, a real Powell.

Years later, as an adult, General Colin Powell often recalled the incident. Sometimes it made him laugh to remember his mistake. Other times he thought about the mark the event had left on him. He had learned about honesty that summer. Honesty wasn't just something he talked about after that. It was something he tried to live by.

It would take years for the world to see and reward the character Colin Powell showed at the camp. For many years, few of his achievements signaled greatness. For many years, he seemed to lack direction. He was not an exceptional student or athlete. Yet his family believed in him and, in their own way, groomed him for greatness.

3

In the Line of Fire

In 1954 Colin graduated from Morris High School. His parents had reason for concern. Colin wasn't an academic star like his sister, Marilyn. Although his attendance was good and he kept up with his homework, he averaged only about a C.

Luther and Arie had not gone past high school themselves. They were working class people who lived by the strength of their hands. Still, they valued education, and there was no question that Colin would go to college somewhere. Times were changing. A college degree was the key to getting a decent job, perhaps in civil service.

Colin wanted to please his parents. After all, they had sacrificed to make his life better. What could he do but try? So he applied to New York University

(NYU) and the City College of New York (CCNY). To his surprise, he was accepted by both.

It was easy to decide between them. The tuition at NYU was $750 a year while only $10 at CCNY. He chose CCNY. It was a college for the children of working class parents. It was inexpensive but not inferior. Its graduates were among the best and the brightest in the world.

Colin found campus life exciting and challenging. His mother suggested that he study engineering. But he quickly found that he didn't do well in the science and math courses required for engineering. He did enjoy geology, though, and eventually majored in that field. As he later explained to his parents, geologists were often employed by oil companies.

But Colin never pursued geology as a career. Instead, he saw something on campus that changed his direction and sparked a lifelong passion. He noticed a number of young men who stood out because of the uniforms they wore. They were part of the Reserve Officers Training Corps (ROTC), an educational program for military officers.

Perhaps because of his admiration for World War II heroes such as Colin Kelly and Audie Murphy, Colin was drawn to the corps. CCNY had the largest group of ROTC cadets in the United States. There were 1,500 on campus. Colin joined army ROTC in the fall of 1954.

Colin joined ROTC during his freshman year in college.

He came to love everything about the program. He looked forward to the drills and the military education. Fairly quickly, he joined a military society (similar to a fraternity) called the Pershing Rifles. That group intensified his love of the military even more.

"For the first time in my life I was a member of a brotherhood," Powell would later say. "The discipline, the structure, the camaraderie, the sense of belonging were what I craved. . . . I found a selflessness within our ranks that reminded me of the caring atmosphere within my family. Race, color, background, income meant nothing."

ROTC graduates are required to serve in the armed forces. They normally enter as officers. Upon graduation from CCNY, Powell became a second lieutenant in the U.S. Army Infantry. He was assigned to a base in Gelnhausen, West Germany.

The soldier's life suited Lieutenant Powell. He was a platoon leader in charge of more than 40 men. He loved the discipline and the sense of fellowship. He loved visiting foreign lands. His one-year service could not have gone better. He was respected and well liked by the other soldiers.

What he disliked was the loneliness. He had been raised in a lively home, where people joked and laughed, grieved and cried with gusto. He missed his family and was happy when he was transferred back to the United States.

He was stationed at Fort Devens, Massachusetts. New York was only a few hours away. He could easily go there on his days off. Colin looked forward to plenty of visits and lots of home cooking.

One weekend, a fellow officer named Michael Hendingburg asked Colin a question. Hendingburg dated a woman in Boston, and she had a roommate, Alma Johnson. Would Colin like to meet Alma and accompany Hendingburg and his girlfriend on a double date?

Red flags went up. The young lieutenant had no interest in blind dates. But Hendingburg wouldn't take no for an answer. Colin finally agreed to the date, but he didn't have high expectations.

Alma Johnson was a graduate student in audiology (speech therapy for the hearing impaired) at Emerson College. A southerner, born and raised in Birmingham, Alabama, she was graceful and kind. She had soft green eyes, brown hair, and a slim build. She was unforgettable.

After their first date, Colin and Alma saw a lot of each other. Alma later said that she had had reservations about dating a military man. But Colin won her over. In turn, she impressed him with her refined intelligence. He felt comfortable talking to her.

They talked about their futures. She talked about her career in audiology. Eventually, they discussed building a life together. Within a year of their meeting, Colin and Alma married on a hot day in Birmingham, August 25, 1962.

The young couple took an apartment in Boston. But after only a few months, Colin was transferred to North Carolina for a five-week training session at Fort Bragg's Unconventional Warfare Center. Soldiers trained at the center could expect assignments in the political hot spots of the world. Just before Christmas, orders came down for Colin to report for duty in Vietnam.

Alma Johnson in her teen years

At that time, the communist governments in the Soviet Union, China, and Cuba were seen as the biggest threats to American interests. Vietnam was another area of military concern. The country had been a French colony before popular resistance forced the French out. At a peace conference with Western powers, Vietnam was given some independence. But the settlement also divided the nation into two parts: North Vietnam, with close ties to the Soviet Union; and South Vietnam, supported by Western nations. As French influence faded in the region, the United States stepped forward to assist the government of the South.

Alma and Colin are married in Birmingham in 1962. Colin's parents are on the left. Alma's parents are on the right.

Although Powell was not surprised when he was ordered to report to Vietnam, his family members were. Like most Americans, they had never heard of the small country on the other side of the world.

Powell was assigned to a force of more than 11,000 American troops. They were not fighting troops but rather advisers to the South Vietnamese. Young Powell had half hoped for an assignment like this. Finally, there'd be an opportunity for some real soldiering.

The order was bittersweet, though. Colin's excitement was tempered by the sadness of leaving his family behind. He would depart two days before Christmas. That alone was enough to take a lot of the joy out of the holiday. But there was more. Alma was pregnant, and Colin's yearlong tour meant he would miss the birth of their first child. The Powells also had the unspoken dread of every military family—that their soldier might die in combat.

Alma knew she would spend many nights worrying about Colin and missing him. But she bore the situation with stoic calm. The orders brought the reality of military life into sharp focus, and she accepted the complications. If Colin was to make a mark in life, he would need the support of his family. Alma was willing to give that. She would live with her parents in Birmingham during his tour.

Colin arrived in Saigon, South Vietnam, on Christmas morning in 1962. The country was lush and green, a land of rice farmers and fishermen that seemed too peaceful and lovely to be a battlefield. But unseen forces were at work—forces that would make this tropical paradise a hellhole of war for decades to come.

Saigon was the capital of South Vietnam. In more peaceful times it had been dubbed "Paris of the Orient." A port city, located at the southern tip of a land mass jutting into the South China Sea, it teemed with people hustling about on foot and in pedal-driven cabs called cyclos. There were fine restaurants and expensive shops. Fashionable women dressed in silk strolled gracefully in the streets.

Powell took in the sights, smells, and sounds of the place for a few days. Within a week, he headed north to a post in a tropical forest along the western border with Laos. A Shau, as the post was called, was situated along a valley that formed a link on the Ho Chi Minh Trail. This vital supply route supported the army of North Vietnam—an army that strongly opposed the American presence in South Vietnam.

The terrain looked like a picture in a travel brochure. It was beautiful, but rugged enough to test every bit of a soldier's physical fitness training. A thick canopy of rain forest covered the land and hid the movements of the enemy.

Powell's job was to advise a South Vietnamese unit. As he understood it, the unit's mission was to slow the flow of men and supplies from North Vietnam. Shortly after arriving in A Shau, Powell realized that the location of the base was unsafe. The enemy could easily launch an attack from the nearby high ground.

Powell asked the Vietnamese commander he was to advise about the location of the outpost. The answer frustrated and confused him. Powell wrote about this exchange in his autobiography:

"What is [the outpost's] mission?" Powell asked Captain Vo Cong Hieu, an easygoing, gentle man, who looked more like a scholar than a soldier.

"Very important outpost," Hieu responded.

"But why is it here?" Powell demanded.

"Outpost is here to protect airfield," Hieu said.

"What's the airfield here for?"

"Airfield here to resupply outpost," Hieu said with a smile. The conversation could have gone around and around like that without end. Powell let the matter drop, but he never forgot the comment.

The United States would fight in Vietnam for another 10 years. War was never officially declared, yet the conflict resulted in the deaths of about 58,000 American soldiers. It bitterly divided the American public, with thousands of young people protesting the war and thousands of draft-age men refusing to fight.

In one way or another, Powell would deal with Vietnam for the next 20 years. During that time, he found no better explanation for U.S. involvement than the circular logic he heard in January 1963. American soldiers were there because they were there because they were there. . . .

The logic may not have seemed real to the soldiers in the field. But the danger was real. Powell's unit was routinely ambushed and often lost men. Most of the time, the soldiers at the head of a column were the ones killed in sniper attacks.

There was never any warning. As the unit patrolled, everything would be calm. The only sounds came from birds high above in the canopy of the forest.

Suddenly, the sound of gunfire would pierce the air. The South Vietnamese could never pinpoint the source of the shooting. By the time they took cover and positioned themselves to return fire, the shooting had stopped and the attackers were gone.

Powell served as an adviser to the South Vietnamese army in 1963.

Powell saw men injured and killed by snipers for a couple of months. It made him mad. How could he fight an enemy that was almost invisible? Even the clothing of the North Vietnamese soldiers was like that of the local people. It was hard to keep soldiers safe.

He thought the men could do more to protect themselves, so he suggested that Captain Hieu order his men to wear bulletproof vests. The Vietnamese officer listened politely each time his American adviser mentioned the idea. He didn't do anything about it, though. Only after Powell repeatedly suggested that the men wear vests did Hieu have some of his men put on the protection. Hieu didn't think the vests would help much. But his opinion soon changed.

On a trail through the forest, the unit was ambushed one day. One of the soldiers wearing a vest was struck in the chest by a bullet. The force knocked him down but didn't kill him.

Powell pried the flattened bullet from the vest and showed it to the other soldiers. The man stood in disbelief, glad to be alive. From that time forward, Hieu and his soldiers had more respect for their American adviser.

The walls of distrust fell away. As they did, Powell learned about the wiry young men with whom he worked. They told him about their lives before the war, their families, and their dreams for the future.

They also gave him a sense of the culture from which they sprang. Powell listened and shared stories of his own life. In the exchange, he learned more about leadership. He learned how to motivate people.

Four months into Powell's tour, his unit started collecting lumber to build a new base. To down the huge trees in the region, the Vietnamese soldiers preferred to use dynamite. But dynamite was in short supply, so Powell had a chain saw flown in.

These troops had other ideas, however. To Powell's shock, he discovered that they were using machine gun fire to take down the trees. Such a waste of ammunition was unthinkable. Had these been American troops, he would have given them an army-style chewing out. But with this group he tried another tack.

Powell waited for the proper moment, then quietly explained to Captain Hieu that the cartridges his men used cost eight cents apiece. The officer estimated the number of bullets it would take to fell one large tree. He thought about the number of trees they had already cut. As he thought and added, the waste of money staggered him. He immediately ordered his men to use saws instead of bullets to cut the trees.

Powell could have simply told Hieu that the actions of his troops were wrong. Instead, Powell gave Hieu the facts he needed to make a wise decision. It became clear to Powell that there was little he couldn't accomplish if he didn't care who got the credit.

Shortly after this incident, Powell suffered a wound that took him out of the combat zone. While on patrol with his unit, he stepped into a *punji* trap. It was a simple booby trap made by placing a sharpened stake, with the point up, into a small, concealed hole. The tip was usually covered with animal dung, which would badly infect any wound the trap might cause.

The wound to Powell's foot was not very serious. Still, it was bad enough for a trip back to Saigon, where he was treated and he recovered with no complications.

Since he was very close to the end of his tour, he did not return to the front lines after the injury. He spent the last weeks at the rear before shipping out to the United States.

★★★★ 4

The Home Front

Colin was happy to be going home. He was eager to see Alma and their son, Michael, who had been born while he was in the field. He was glad to leave the fighting in Southeast Asia. But Colin found himself in the midst of another sort of war zone in the United States.

For years, the American South had been segregated. Blacks couldn't attend school with whites. They weren't allowed in many restaurants and stores. Interracial marriages were banned. Often, blacks weren't allowed to vote.

During Colin's absence, the Civil Rights movement had gone into high gear. Martin Luther King and other black leaders were challenging segregation and demanding equality for black people.

But the whites who enforced segregation were not going to give up without a fight. They responded to Civil Rights protests with acts of terrorism. They bombed black homes and churches, lynched and murdered some protesters, and theatened many others.

It angered Powell to think that while he was serving his country, his country did little to secure the rights and safety of his people. Even his fellow army officers showed signs of racism. Once, shortly after Powell returned to the United States, he was confronted by a white officer who complained about the Civil Rights protests. The officer didn't think that the government should require white-owned stores, hotels, and restaurants to serve black people.

"I told [him] how it was trying to find a decent place to eat on the road in the South, or a motel where you, your wife, and your kid could stay," Powell later recalled. ". . . . Medgar Evers of the NAACP [National Association for the Advancement of Colored People] had been murdered the year before in Mississippi. Sheriff Bull Connor had set police dogs against people. Murderers had blown up four children in a Birmingham church. And these people were arguing about 'property rights'!"

Powell was stationed at Fort Benning in Georgia, in the heart of the Old South. Most white people in the region strongly supported segregation. When Powell left the base, he was often the target of racial slurs. The army, however, was integrated and less charged with racial hatred. On the base, African American families did not experience the worst of the racist acts.

Alma with five-year-old Michael and three-year-old Linda in 1968

On the whole, the army was a good place to raise a family. In 1965 Alma and Colin added to theirs. Linda, their second child, was born that year. Colin had a happy family life and continued to make progress in his career.

By 1967 he had completed the Infantry Officers Advanced Course and had entered the Army Command and General Staff College at Fort Leavenworth, Kansas. Moving to Kansas brought the stresses of packing and unpacking. But it was a small inconvenience. Overall, army life treated Colin Powell well.

Powell had been away from Vietnam nearly five years when he drew the assignment again. By the time he returned in July 1968, the country had changed drastically. The streets of Saigon were clogged with jeeps and army trucks. There was also a different mood among the soldiers. Powell noticed the change right away when he got to his base at Duc Pho, a half-hour helicopter ride from the coastal city of Chu Lai.

What he saw shocked him. As he stepped off the helicopter, he nearly tripped over crates of ammunition, left rusting in haphazard piles. A stench hung in the air from the open latrines. The American soldiers were dirty and undisciplined.

By 1969 the United States had about 540,000 troops in Vietnam. Americans were no longer just advisers. They were now combatants. Though U.S. forces hadn't lost much territory, they still felt a sense of defeat. The feelings grew even stronger when the soldiers returned to the United States to face angry antiwar protestors. Powell felt the military leadership had failed these soldiers.

"These were good men, the same kind of young Americans who had fought, bled, and died winning victory after victory throughout our country's history," Powell wrote. "They were no less brave or skilled, but by this time in the war, they lacked inspiration and a sense of purpose."

Powell, now a major, was not to stay long with the battalion. He was quickly brought into the inner circle of commanders who planned the war in his sector. Still, that first image stayed in his mind through the rest of the tour. "If we're going to send young men and women into harm's way," he said, "we have to make sure that they have a clear purpose that they're fighting for... and that the American people understand that purpose and that the American people are supporting them in what they do."

Before leaving Vietnam, Powell applied to graduate school at George Washington University in Washington, D.C. He learned in June 1969 that he had been accepted into the School of Government and Business Administration. He hung up his uniform and stepped back into civilian life for two years.

During Colin's second tour in Vietnam, Alma and the children had lived in Birmingham. Upon Colin's return, the family moved to a house in Woodbridge, Virginia, a surburb of Washington. In May 1970, a second daughter, Annemarie, was born.

Powell adjusted well to life at George Washington University. He liked the free exchange of ideas. He liked discussing the "whys" in decision making as well as the "whats." He also spent a lot of time reflecting on American involvement in Vietnam. His own disappointment about the government's handling of the war was amplified by the ongoing debate on campus.

The conservatives who supported the war and the liberals who opposed it hurled angry words back and forth. Powell listened and considered the debate. What he heard bothered him deeply. He was a military man who was happy with his career. But some criticisms of the military were true.

After earning a master's degree in business administration in 1971, Powell reported for duty at the Pentagon, headquarters for the Department of Defense. He looked forward to the discipline of army life, but was surprised to discover a military establishment under siege. Complaints about American involvement in Vietnam echoed in nearly every newspaper in the land.

Military leaders could not help being affected. They thought about change—about making the military more efficient and effective. In one of Powell's first assignments at the Pentagon, he was asked to produce a report about cutting the size of the army from 1.6 million soldiers to just 500,000.

Powell did not stay at that job long. At the insistence of his superiors, he applied to become a White House Fellow. The fellowship program was designed to develop future leaders. It involved advanced training at the highest level of government. Powell was accepted into the program in 1972.

Lessons in Leadership

Powell's yearlong White House Fellowship gave him a rare insider's view of the federal government. Because he had a business degree, he was assigned to the Office of Management and Budget. This quiet office was actually one of the most powerful in Washington. It controlled the purse strings of the other departments.

Other graduate students read books about the political system. But as a White House Fellow, Powell saw the cogs and gears at work. He discussed presidential power with Richard Nixon and laws with members of Congress.

In January 1973, Powell and the other fellows took a trip to the Soviet Union and Eastern Europe. Powell relished the chance to meet new people and hear new ideas.

The White House Fellowship exposed Powell to the inner workings of government.

It was an exciting time. But, in the end, Powell longed for the life of a soldier. As a lieutenant colonel, he sought to lead troops. In the spring of 1973, he asked the army for a command of his own. There was no guarantee he'd get one, since positions were based on availability and army politics. Still, he tried and hoped.

He wound up assigned to Korea, as commander of an infantry battalion. Had he a choice, Powell would have preferred another assignment. It was an "unac-companied tour," which meant a year's separation from his family. It would be his third separation from ten-year-old Michael, his second from eight-year-old Linda, and his first from three-year-old Annemarie.

Alma was not pleased. Still, she supported her husband. Colin did not take the decision to leave lightly. He hated to say goodbye to Alma, a trusted counselor and friend as well as a cherished companion. There were opportunities for him in Washington. The Office of Management and Budget wanted him to stay another year. He and Alma considered the offer.

The assignment in Korea was a sacrifice all the way around. But Colin and Alma decided it was the best career choice. Colin would not advance further in the army if he stayed in Washington, they reasoned.

So Powell headed to Korea, part of a force sent to maintain the 1953 truce between North Korea and South Korea, established at the end of the Korean War. This assignment would prove to be Powell's most important lesson in military leadership. His teacher would be his commanding officer, Major General Henry E. "the Gunfighter" Emerson.

Emerson was a tall, rugged man of about 50, whose intense gaze and hooked nose made him look like a bird of prey. From the first, Powell liked Emerson's incredible energy. When addressing his staff during regular meetings, Emerson was like a preacher. He always thundered to a close with the same phrase: "If you don't do your jobs right, soldiers won't win."

Powell inherited a battalion that was like many army units of the time. Many of the soldiers, drafted out of poor neighborhoods during a massive military buildup in the late 1960s, had marginal skills. They lacked discipline and distrusted authority. There were racial tensions and drug abuse. The army was still reeling from the failures of Vietnam.

Morale was bad, as Powell discovered within days of his arrival. It was a cold night, and Powell bundled up and walked to the office of the provost marshal—head of the military police.

As Powell entered an office that contained detention cells, he walked in on a fight. A half-dozen or so military police officers (MPs) battled to subdue one soldier. With some difficulty, they shackled him and wrestled him into a van.

Powell learned that the soldier was part of a conspiracy to murder the provost marshal. The plan had been foiled, and no one had been injured. But the incident opened Powell's eyes to problems in the armed forces. He was convinced that things had to change. General Emerson was also committed to improving morale. He found a kindred spirit in Lieutenant Colonel Powell, or "Bro P" as the black troops called him.

The nickname Bro P came out of an encounter with a young black soldier near the company recreation room. The man was out of control. His eyes were fire red. Powell could tell that the soldier was either drunk or drugged. The pool cue he held like a club was at the ready.

Powell in Korea, 1974

"Somebody's gonna die!" the soldier bellowed. "You put my buddy in jail. Nobody's gonna put me in jail. Somebody's gonna die first!"

Powell weighed his options. The MPs had been contacted. He could wait and let them wrestle the man to the ground and carry him away in chains. But Powell thought there might be another, more dignified, way. He stepped forward. He addressed the soldier in a gentle voice:

"Son, put the cue down."

"No, Sir."

"Do you know who I am?"

"Yes, Sir, Colonel Powell."

Powell came closer. He continued in a calm, quiet voice: "I want you to put the cue down before you hurt somebody. I want you to put it down before somebody hurts you. You see, if you don't do what I tell you, all these men are going to whip hell out of you. Then, when they're done, you're going to the stockade for a year. What sense does that make? So put the cue down, and we'll have a nice talk."

Suddenly, the man dropped the cue and broke down in tears. The confrontation was over. He was placed on restriction for several weeks and soon was back on regular duty. Powell passed the reformed soldier one day and heard him remark to his buddies: "That's Bro P, Brother Powell, he's all right."

Powell's actions had kept the soldier from a dishonorable discharge. Powell had not only salvaged the man's military life but he had also salvaged a good soldier for the army. The fact that the young man was black was certainly a source of pride for Powell. He knew the value of looking out for one's own. The black troops in his command seemed to feel pride in Powell's achievements, too.

In turn, Powell took pride in serving directly under a black general, Brigadier General Harry Brooks, the assistant division commander. Powell admired Brooks's stability, coolness, and common sense. He was part of a long line of distinguished black military men.

Powell depended on that line and hoped to leave a firm foundation for future generations of black soldiers. He was beloved by the black troops. But he didn't let this fact go to his head. He never forgot his duty as an army officer and, as they say in the street, "he didn't take no mess." When the situation demanded it, Powell could be very strict. Years later, he wrote in his autobiography:

> Among the blacks, I had some of the finest soldiers and NCOs [noncommissioned officers] I have ever known. They had found in the army a freedom in which they could fulfill themselves. I did not like seeing their proud performance tarnished by nihilistic types, a minority within a minority. What problem soldiers needed, like the kid with the pool cue, was someone to care about them....I wanted to care for them positively.

At the end of the yearlong tour, Powell found that he had grown as an officer. He had always been efficient. But now he had a deeper understanding of how to motivate the soldiers in his command. General Emerson recognized that Powell had the ability to be a top commander. In fact, Emerson recommended Powell as general material. That recommendation would add steam to a career that was already moving fast.

Powell talks to soldiers in his command during a field training exercise at Fort Campbell, Kentucky.

★ ★ ★ ★ 6

Stepping Stones to Power

With the rank and record to make him the envy of many older officers, Powell returned to the United States in 1974. He was slated to attend the National War College at Fort McNair in Washington, D.C.

The War College has been called the Yale or Harvard of the military educational system. Only 140 slots .are available each year, and acceptance is a great honor. Powell looked at his admission as a chance to further sharpen his skills. He began classes in the fall of 1975. It was a good time to be at the college.

Questions swirled everywhere. What had gone wrong in Vietnam? What had gone wrong with the presidency of Richard Nixon, who had been forced to resign in 1974? What's wrong? What's wrong?

The country was looking inward and trying to plot a new course. College campuses were alive with fiery discussions and bold new thoughts. The War College was no exception. Powell loved the feel of college life again.

One of the most valuable experiences he had there was exposure to the writings of a 19th-century Prussian military man named Karl von Clausewitz. More than one hundred years earlier, Clausewitz had written: "No one starts a war, or rather no one in his senses should do so, without first being clear in his mind what he intends to achieve by that war and how he intends to achieve it." Clausewitz also wrote that leaders must set a war's objectives, while armies must achieve the objectives.

These two ideas would shape Powell's style as he moved up the ranks to the highest levels of military and government power. He graduated from the National War College in 1976, confident that he was ready to lead the military into a new era.

That year, he was promoted to full colonel. With that rank he served at Fort Campbell, Kentucky, and in the administration of President Jimmy Carter. He worked as the special assistant to the deputy secretary of defense before he was promoted to brigadier general in 1979.

During the eight-year administration of President Ronald Reagan (1980–1988), Powell served in several military and government positions, including senior military assistant to the secretary of defense and national security adviser. He was involved in the 1983 invasion of the Caribbean island of Grenada, where the United States feared a Cuban-sponsored takeover. In 1986 Powell was a central planner in the bombing of Libya, a country that had supported terrorism in the Middle East and Europe. Powell watched the military grow and change. His experiences would serve him well as he stepped into a new role in a new presidential administration.

In October 1989, President George Bush appointed Colin Powell chairman of the Joint Chiefs of Staff.

Secretary of Defense Dick Cheney, President George Bush, and JCOS Chairman Colin Powell

The Joint Chiefs of Staff is made up of the heads of the army, navy, marines, and air force. The chairman commands the armed forces on behalf of the president and the secretary of defense.

Powell's appointment was a historic moment. At age 52, he was the youngest chairman ever. He was the first African American to get the job and the only person who had not attended the U.S. Military Academy or the U.S. Naval Academy.

Bush had passed over more experienced officers to make the choice. Some of the president's advisers said that Powell wasn't ready for such an important position. They feared that other senior commanders might not want to follow Powell—that they might even resent him.

Their objections made some sense. But in other ways, Bush thought the advisers were dead wrong. A close look at Powell's accomplishments made it clear to President Bush that Colin Powell was the right man for the job.

Powell had risen through the military ranks by merit. He was never given a promotion as a political favor. Through hard work and brain power, he had earned every stripe, bar, and star he wore. Even his critics struggled to find fault with him. He had a gift for working with others and understood politics as well as anyone in government. He had won high praise as a warrior in Vietnam.

Powell was modest about his achievements and always said that they were not his alone. He stressed that he stood on the shoulders of those who came before him, particularly black soldiers who had endured racism and segregation in the past. By fighting for equality, these soldiers had given Powell the chance to go as far as his talents allowed.

"To some extent, I'm flattered that most people almost don't think of me as a black chairman of the Joint Chiefs of Staff anymore and that's good," Powell said in an interview late in his career. "That shows that America is progressing. But at the same time, I let everybody know that I know I'm the first black chairman of the JCOS and hope that that gives encouragement to some young African American in an inner city somewhere . . . not to be constrained. If I could do it, they can do it."

Powell understood the importance of good role models. He praised the courage and patriotism of the all-black 54th Massachusetts Volunteers, a unit that was virtually wiped out in a charge on a Confederate stronghold during the Civil War. He respected the "Buffalo Soldiers," the black Tenth Cavalry troops of the Old West. His other heroes included Lieutenant Henry O. Flipper, a member of the Tenth Cavalry and the first black person to graduate from the U.S. Military Academy; Brigadier General Benjamin O. Davis of World War II, the first black army general;

and General Daniel "Chappie" James of the Vietnam era, the first black to reach the four-star rank.

They had opened the doors through which Powell walked. They had set the standard of excellence that had guided his career. Inspired by those men, he felt prepared for any and all challenges.

These challenges came quickly. In late 1989, Powell planned an invasion of Panama. The action was brief and successful. General Manuel Noriega, charged with allowing drugs to pass through Panama to the United States, was overthrown.

The next year, the government of the Soviet Union started falling apart. Suddenly, the Cold War—the hostility between the United States and the communist Soviet Union—was over. The biggest American enemy for almost fifty years was no longer a military threat.

Americans demanded a reduction in military spending. Congress responded to the call by proposing cuts in the military budget. Powell had to make sure the cuts did not weaken the armed forces. Instead, he moved to create a leaner, more efficient military.

Had Powell simply helped downsize the military, his chairmanship may have been historic but not memorable. We remember soldiers for the wars they fight. The war for which Colin Powell will be remembered is the one in the Persian Gulf against Iraq.

Center of the Storm

Early in the morning of August 2, 1990, 80,000 Iraqi troops crossed the border into the small, oil-rich nation of Kuwait. The invasion came after decades of disputes between the two countries. President Saddam Hussein, leader of Iraq, ordered the attack, claiming Kuwait was Iraqi territory.

No other governments recognized the claim, and the United Nations (UN) demanded that Iraq remove its forces from its neighbor's soil. Hussein would not budge, saying Kuwait had wrongly been separated from his country when European colonial powers re-drew the map of the Middle East at the end of World War I. Hussein's invading forces took full control of the tiny nation while the world watched.

Powell discusses the U.S. mission in Iraq at a January 1991 press briefing.

Government leaders, particularly those from neighboring Arab countries, tried to talk Hussein into releasing the territory. He stubbornly refused. So the leaders tried another tack.

The United Nations declared an economic boycott. Countries were instructed not to do business with Iraq. By cutting off trade, the UN hoped to hurt the

Iraqi economy and pressure Hussein to pull his troops out of Kuwait.

Like many people, Powell hoped the boycott would work. He was reluctant to pursue a military solution. But time was running out. As the leaves of fall dropped from the trees in Washington, it became clear to President Bush that Saddam Hussein would have to be forced out of Kuwait. Bush instructed Powell to plan an attack that would involve American soldiers as well as troops from allied countries.

Positions on both sides continued to harden. Finally, on November 29, the United Nations authorized the use of force if Iraq did not withdraw from Kuwait by January 15, 1991.

The United States was expected to take the lead if and when fighting began. But that would put young American men and women in danger. That was not something that Colin Powell would do lightly. American lives were too important. It was a lesson learned from Vietnam he would never forget.

"War should be the politics of last resort," Powell said. "When we go to war, we should have a purpose that our people understand and support."

Powell spent much of the fall of 1990 helping members of Congress understand the situation in the Persian Gulf. The task was not easy. As Americans watched the buildup of forces in the Persian Gulf, fears of another Vietnam War surfaced. Congress members and the public worried about the loss of American lives.

Powell understood these concerns. He even shared some of them. Still, he was there to serve the president. He took care to speak to every fear. In the end, he convinced Congress that the use of overwhelming force would most likely bring the war to a swift conclusion. On January 12, 1991, Congress approved the use of American troops in an offensive plan called Operation Desert Storm.

The January 15 deadline for Hussein to pull back his forces came and went. On January 17, 1991, bombing raids began. For more than a month, United States and United Nations aircraft pounded bridges, artillery, and Iraqi troops. Most of Iraq's planes were grounded or destroyed. Most of its supply depots lay in shambles.

With the enemy reeling from the air attacks, ground forces moved in on February 24. American, French, Egyptian, and Syrian forces closed in on the Iraqi forces remaining in Kuwait. On February 27, allied forces reclaimed the capital of Kuwait City. By February 28, the war was over.

Operation Desert Storm was a stunning success. With it, the United States threw off the embarrassment of the Vietnam War. Colin Powell—along with General Norman Schwarzkopf, commander of the U.S. forces—stepped into the history books.

Colin Powell and Norman Schwarzkopf emerged as heroes of the Persian Gulf War.

Powell continued as the chairman of the Joint Chiefs of Staff until his retirement in 1993. He oversaw further downsizing of the military and dealt with controversies such as whether or not gay soldiers would be allowed to serve. The image that would remain foremost in American minds, however, would be that of the triumphant hero.

"There's nothing mystical about it," he said on the eve of his retirement. "I've tried to do my job to the best of my ability. I've tried to give solid advice to secretaries of state and the presidents I've worked for. And I've tried to do my best serving the men and women of the armed services."

In 1995 *My American Journey* was published. It became an immediate best-seller. Powell toured the country to promote the book. People looked toward the 1996 presidential elections, and many suggested Powell as a potential candidate.

Powell signs copies of his autobiography, *My American Journey,* at a Washington, D.C., bookstore in December 1995.

When he announced that he would not run for office, he explained: "I will remain in private life and seek other ways to serve. I have a deep love for this country that has no bounds. I will find other ways to contribute to the important work needed to keep us moving forward."

What will he do? Will he run for president in the future? His honesty and integrity have won him the support of millions, which would give him a strong base if he decides to enter politics.

In retirement, Powell has more time to pursue a hobby, repairing vintage cars, and more time to spend with his wife and children. He and Alma are also proud to be grandparents. The youngest Powell, Michael's son, is Jeffrey Michael Powell.

Powell keeps busy. He frequently speaks to business and youth groups. When he talks to young people, he stresses the importance of education.

The journey of Colin Powell has been fruitful and filled with triumph and joy. He has gone places he could not have imagined as a child in the Bronx. He has served the United States with distinction. Still, the story of this hero is not over. He has merely turned a new page.

Bibliography

Means, Howard. Colin Powell: *Soldier/Statesman— Statesman/Soldier.* New York: Donald I. Fine, 1993.

Powell, Colin, and Joseph E. Persico. *My American Journey.* New York: Random House, 1995.

Roth, David. *Sacred Honor: A Biography of Colin Powell.* Grand Rapids, Mich.: Zondervan Publishing and Harper San Francisco, 1993.

Woodward, Bob. *The Commanders.* New York: Simon and Schuster, 1991.

Index

ABOUT THE AUTHOR

Reggie Finlayson is a modern-day griot—an oral historian of the West African tradition. In this role, he combines poetry, music, and storytelling to preserve the history of African and African American people.

Finlayson studied at Swarthmore College and at Marquette University, where he earned a master's degree in journalism. He is a member of the Ko-Thi African Dance Company and a teacher at the Milwaukee Area Technical College. He has written six plays, one of which is for children. This is his first nonfiction book for young readers.

ACKNOWLEDGMENTS

Photographs reproduced with permission of Reuters/Archive Photos: p.1; UPI/Corbis-Bettmann: pp. 2, 51; U.S. Army: pp. 6 (Russ Roederer), 48; Archive Photos/Consolidated News: p. 8; Reuters/Corbis-Bettmann: p. 11; General Powell's personal collection: pp. 12, 16, 23, 26, 27, 31, 37, 45; U.S Government: p. 42; Corbis-Bettmann: pp. 56, 59; AFP Corbis-Bettmann: p. 60.

Front cover: Reuters/Vidal Medina/Archive Photos
Back cover: Archive Photos/Consolidated News

FREEPORT MEMORIAL LIBRARY

‖‖‖‖‖‖‖

J
B
Powell
F

Finlayson, Reggie.

Colin Powell.

DATE			

FREEPORT MEMORIAL LIBRARY
CHILDREN'S ROOM

BAKER & TAYLOR